The First Blast to Awaken Women Degenerate

The First Blast to Awaken Women Degenerate

Rachel McCrum

**FREIGHT
BOOKS**

First published 2017

Freight Books
49–53 Virginia Street
Glasgow, G1 1TS
www.freightbooks.co.uk

A CIP catalogue reference for this book is available from the British
Library.

ISBN 978-1-911332-42-8

Typeset by Freight in Plantin
Printed and Bound in Poland by Hussar Books

the publisher acknowledges investment from
Creative Scotland toward the publication of this book

Rachel McCrum was born in 1982 and grew up in Donaghadee, Northern Ireland. She has a BA in English Literature and Language from Jesus College, Oxford. She has previously published two pamphlets with Stewed Rhubarb Press: *The Glassblower Dances* (2012) and *Do Not Alight Here Again* (2015). She lived in Edinburgh, Scotland from 2010 to 2016 where she was the Broad of cult spoken word cabaret Rally & Broad, the inaugural BBC Scotland Poet in Residence and a recipient of an RLS Fellowship in 2016. She now lives in Montreal, Quebec.

Contents

Broad

Dark in a Belfast sweatbox,
a country voice, slurred and steaming,
dove into my ear.

Jaysus. You're a hefty one.
I believe it was a compliment
he thought he paid.

These shoulders are broad.
My mother was a farmer's daughter with a voice
that stretched across three fields.

From her I gained
blue eyes, child-bearing hips
and feet planted family tree trunk to the ground.

From her I learned
that self-indulgence is a dirty word.
That it is important to get the potatoes

on the table for your brothers
before you write the application
for the university.

She did both.
The first in the family
to live by words

rather than by hands
and she grew, along the way,
uncharacteristically quiet.

It can be hard
to explain the weight
of paper.

In the church hall
after my great-grandmother's funeral
they turn over my palms

as they clasp my forearms
to see if I have yet managed
an honest day's work.

I have only one callus to show them.
The indentation between the knuckles
of the middle finger of my right hand.

I go sailing

for Margarida Jorge

Last summer, my father and I made
the North Sea crossing.
Inverness spat us out the Moray Firth
crested by bullying dolphins.

The first day saw us breathless
over swift clean waves,
racing between oil platforms
because we knew how to ride the wind.

The second day
our stomachs dropped
as the sea rose up
to meet us.

A heightening gale,
the pitch and maw of big water.

I held the helm for ten hours
cold, wet and muscles biting.
He, sixteen stone of bad hip,
did what he had to.

Tying and retying salted sheets
reefing canvas pulling fat with wind
and with one fretting lifeline
straining him to the foredeck.

Never so glad to see the sea
give up a sullen coastline.
In the harbour, we shoved
cheese rolls in our mouths sideways

and did not mention the crossing.
But after, ravelling up the family knot
I heard him tell my mother
she kept her steady.

Months later, landsick
and tethered to the corners of my bed,
I fret over disappointment,
yet another wayward change of course.

He sends a message

signed off *Your proud da*

and I, like any daughter would,
– like any child would –
cry in the rented privacy
of a lurching room.

Problems to Sharpen the Young (i)

Wife says to husband *We must cross this water*
Husband says to wife *We cannot afford a bigger boat*
Daughter says to mother *We are strong enough*
Brother says to sister *We must stay together*

Sister says to father *The boat is big enough for two little ones*
Mother says to son *Zip up your pullover tightly*
Brother says to sister *It's a long way to row*
Father says to daughter *Remember what I taught you*

Mother says to daughter *Keep the second star on your right*
Daughter says to mother *I will come back for you*
Father says to son *You will have to stay alone*
Son says to father *Who will look after me?*

Sister and brother make the first crossing.
Daughter returns alone.
Son remains alone.
Mother takes the boat over.
Son returns alone.
Sister and brother make the second crossing.
Mother and son are reunited.
Daughter takes boat back.
Father takes the boat over alone.
Daughter remains alone.
Son makes the final crossing solo.
For the third and final time, sister and brother make the crossing
    together.
Family is reunited, exhausted, muscles straining stronger.
None of them have papers. The context is irrelevant.

Who wants a home?

Hands up!
Heads down!
Don't look us in the eye!

Who wants a home?
We do.
Do not have children. Insulate yourself against such leaks.

Who wants a home?
We do.
Lower your chattering voices. Do not take up so much space.

Who wants a home?
We do.
Turnaround. We have no room here. Find your own.

We do.
Any old roof will do.
One that does not
billow, fold or falter,
get soggy when it rains,
would be nice
but we'll take anything
we can call our own.

We do.
We remember the houses we visited as children.
The scent of good china and dust, potted palms
that had lived for jungle ages.
Extra chairs for visiting aunts and…
we thought we'd grow up in houses like this.
We thought we'd grow up.
Where are our paint samples
and our permanence?
Our trips to buy grout?

We do.
We teetering ones,
short sighted, feckless,
reckless and callow.

Is this really our fault
our squints, our greying hairs,
our failing energy, our fear?

Radio Orkney

The sea, trailing white ghost hair, shivers home in waves,
to a population modest, low voiced, unfixed in stone.

A surge of Old Scotia that foams and waves
from south and west, the incomers in.

The join where Balfour's whitewashed roof braves
the ossuary absent of bones, the fingers of the setting sun.

A groundswell sweet and low as local airwaves
flies like a crow between dry walls and standing stones.

A surge along the length of waves.
Maxwell's sums still standing strong.

The island living new tradition. Soundwaves
longer than light and nothing's set in stone.

No tick needed, nothin missin here. Lambs shiver and brave
standing tall. The rise and fall of speech. Nothin set in stone.

Do not alight here again

The best time – those ten minutes before the wheels unlock,
the view from the air giving the lie to the land.

Hold hot gritted eyes wide for the curve of hills.
Drink the ragged shrug of wavelets racing from the shore.

Drag foamlines over uneasy glassine water with a fingernail,
then dig deep to the palm. And yet –

craving the illicit place still. From our childhood windows,
on clear days, we could see the Mainland

where we were always supposed to end up.
A boot to the backside when we came of age –

Get out.
Leave while you can.

Exile yourselves.
Make your accent vagrant.

Untether your compass.
Entertain Portuguese notions.

Wander far.
Be better than us.

Do not alight here again.

Problems to Sharpen the Young (ii)

So. There's this farmer,
and he has a fox and a goose
and a big green cabbage.

Why does a farmer have a fox?
That's not important.
It doesn't have to be a fox.
It could be a wolf and a pig and a bag of beans.
A panther, a pigeon, a pot of porridge.
Coyote, chicken, corn.
What's important is
who eats who.

Who does eat who?
Fox eats goose.
Goose eats cabbage.
If left to their own devices.

Why?
Because that's the way it is. So.
There's this farmer. And there's a boat.

How big is the boat?
Never big enough.
There's a boat, and it's blue,
and there's a body of water.

What sort of water?
A river, fast and deep
with crocodiles.
Yes. There are crocodiles
so they cannot swim across.
The farmer
the fox
and the goose.

And the cabbage.
And the cabbage.
All of them have arrived
at the bank of the river.

Where did they come from?
From home.

Where are they going?
To the other side.

Why?
Because the grass is greener there.
And there's a troll under the bridge.

There's a bridge?
Yes but they can't use the bridge.
They must use the boat
to get to the other side.
Cross the water
in the boat that is blue.

What's the question again?
The question is
one of appetite.

The question is who
must move the most.

And the answer is the goose.
Why must the goose
travel so far?

Wrong. The answer cannot be gauged
until we know the final resting place.

The goose never moved.
He's just spinning in his grave.

Unbuilding a house

I am unbuilding a house.
Across the living room floor, bricks lie rubbled.

Each morning without fail I carefully stub
my toes, cursing ferociously and quietly

(today I damned
my grandmother).

Then, limping and trailing a damson smear,
I heft a brick into each hand

rub the skin raw from my palms
choke on dust

and lumber out to the street.
My pyjamas are ripped.

The road outside my house
is becoming cluttered with rocks.

I have tried to line them neatly
along the gutter

thinking that they may be of use
to someone someplace.

Bricks, even those with small plum smudges,
may be used to build again.

Or perhaps, I worry later,
someone will use these rocks as weapons.

A conveniently sized grab for rage
perhaps a fist sized resistance

hurled against riot shields
or just launched with an irresistible
pissed-up urge to shatter windscreens.

Runaways

For Matthew

Our finest hour turned grim
at the speed of light,
and it's dig-in or flee.
A desperate abdication,
this wilful taste
for the changing of constellations.

Meanwhile, my brother searches for celestial runaways.
When duelling galaxies clash with enough violence,
some bodies, willing or not, are flung out solo.

Stripped of the collective energy, wandering and rogue,
they glow too faintly to be seen
against the masses still holding strong.
Get lost against the blare of the crowd.

Look harder. There is more in the sky
than you see at first glance.
Between the galaxies, light seeps.

Tomato Sonata

In the suburbs of a grey city low
lying and laid low – 70s Belfast –
a sight to make even the coppers laugh.
A DIY giant red tomato,
happily, placidly blocking the crossroads.
Magnificent garish refusal, one
plastic resistance held against the done
thing. Contact point. An eight-foot mischief-show.
Of all the trips I make back – in spirit –
home, it's this absurd pneumatic beacon,
this implacable comedy, this thing,
that reminds me as we click rage and spit
pixels of fruitless ire and ego –
not only those with loudest voices sing.

I lost my shoes on Rachel Street

I lost my shoes on Rachel St.
Head lolled back to rest
against the pillow of the Mont
kiss the foot of the electric cross
tongue kinked, jawbone clattering
to the pneumatic dentistry on Saint Denis.

I lost my grip on Rachel St.
The length of me flopped
to smother the aloof and watchful city,
my arms heat-heavy bisected the grid,
wrists came to rest on fretful bridges.
I thrust my hands to trail
the sludge of the river bottom,
rested my ankles between the railroad tracks,
rolled dust
between the enormous cratered blisters on my toes.

I lost my skirt on Rachel St.
The breeze whipped it
as in the slipstream of a passing skater
as his fingers edged under the hem
violating as a muttered curse.
I watched it float softly across the highway
where every town genuflects down.
Took a shine to the church's thrust,
considered commerce's glint,
but in the end took the Olympic Stadium
as a lover
ever the sacred athletic aesthetic
perfected performance of the wordless flesh preferred.

Speak they whispered on Rachel St
but a dog had run away with my tongue.
The city, the shape of a kiss, an open mouth,
and I unable to name my neck from my ass.

All summer long I lay on Rachel St
my raw elbows twisting to touch treetops
stuck high and dry on sidestreets.
I winked at traffic lights, shook creamy thighs
to the wind up wail of the firetrucks.

Speak! they commanded on Rachel St

as the ducks drifted silent and unified as iron filings.
In the park gullible yahoos googled me digital –
could never snap me all at once,
the whale balloon tethered
the ballet of the open mouth moving

SPEAK! they howled on Rachel St.
I licked my salty lips
mouthed silent curses
these fat and heavy words
that filled the mouth with spit
but nothing uttered.

All summer long, I lay on Rachel St,
as horses tramped through my hair,
as carpenter ants, raccoons, scurried
out of the warm hairy musk of my nostrils,
the moist nest of my armpits
used for the meetings of clandestine lovers –

SPEAAAKKKKKK! they screamed on Rachel St
fire hydrants exploded with joy
spilt their strawberry load

and still
and still
stuttered –
gasped –

gaped –
no words
no words
no language

falling between meanings
like cracks in the tarmac –

So piece by piece on Rachel St
they stripped me for spectacle.
Magpied me.
Pulled out my hair to stuff
winter jackets, jacked up my teeth
for paving slabs, lashed my skin to ribbons
for balcony umbrellas, toenails for boat races,

and my eardrums extracted for the tamtams weekly prayer

I lost my name on Rachel St.

My wallet.
My work ethic.
My virtue.
My childhood fears.
My tongue.
My tongue.
My tongue

began to move to flick when
everything else was nearly gone
and we had been silent long enough
the ones who lay heavy in the street
on Rachel St we dug in our heels

we lumbered to our feet on Rachel St
kicked aside the railway tracks
and on Rachel St we lifted our tongues
we opened our mouths
SPEEEEEEAAAAAAAAAAAAAAAAKKKKKKKKKKKKKKKK!

we roared
and with those waves of sound
we tilted the city
cetacean gulping
we sank the silence.

The five o'clock poem

This is the five o'clock poem.
Good evening.

Almost everything that has happened today
is in the five o'clock poem.

Trust in its being the truth.
This is the five o'clock poem.

The five o'clock poem began somewhere sometime ago.
The five o'clock poem has been scooped and hacked.

All jargon has been removed from the five o'clock poem.
The five o'clock poem has been meticulously researched.

The reporter has recorded a feature on the five o'clock poem.
The editor has sighed over the five o'clock poem.

The five o'clock poem has been torn from typewriters and tape.
A webpage has been produced about the five o'clock poem.

But first, the five o'clock poem.

Downing Street has denied the five o'clock poem.
Video footage has emerged of the five o'clock poem.
Police have raided the headquarters of the five o'clock poem.
The Education Secretary has announced the testing of the five
    o'clock poem.
The death has been announced of the five o'clock poem.

This has been the five o'clock poem.
Good evening.

Problems to Sharpen the Young (iii)

In the middle of the night, Alice, Beth, Charley and Dan are running hard. Presently, they come to a narrow and fragile wooden bridge.

They must cross this bridge. They must use a torch when crossing it, to avoid falling through the rotten and missing planks. The bridge can only hold two persons at any one time.

Luckily, everyone is about the same weight but some are faster than others. The hounds of hell are gaining and will be ripping open tendons in 15 minutes time.

Alice can cross the bridge in 1 minute.
Beth can cross the bridge in 2 mins.
Charley can cross the bridge in 5mins.
Dan can cross the bridge in 8 mins.

Answer the following questions.
1. Why are they running? Have they done something wrong? Should they be caught?
2. Why is Dan so slow? Does Dan deserve to cross the bridge?
3. Why has the bridge not been repaired properly before it was allowed to fall into such a state? Whose responsibility is the bridge?
4. Why are Alice and Beth so fast? Should they just save themselves? Do they deserve it?
5. Should they all turn to fight the dogs?
6. Whose need to cross is greatest?
7. Whose teeth are sharpest?

Ling Chi

Sometimes they start with the eyes
to spare the shame.

The contentious use of opiates to distance pain.
Some say a honeyed absence corrupts what dignity is left.
Some. Not those facing the cleaver, I'd bet.

The merciful kill quick.
A single deep pierce
to the heart-chamber.

The postmortem pics
show the blood-flow stopped
well before the cuts would cease.

Thick slow clots
sticking to what is left of skin
refusing to soak back to earth.

slice by slice by
sting by sting by
flesh by flesh by

An ankle bone gone now, or rib.
Buttock or breast. Shoulderblade.
What next for the carvery?

Who will dare to pull the emperor from his horse?
What voice from the crowd will first shout
Stop, for the love of all that is good, stop.

For the want of a nail

tied to the string of a single silver balloon
hoarded then released each noon
one unequal opposing point of contact
for the pinprick hope in a million
that it might cause the sky to fall.

The Official Line

Give it the old…

…heave ho boys!

The blindest eye ever turned

[quick, call the zoologists]

to disrupt-distort-disorder

…the official line

oh
giraffe me
jaguar me
zebra me fleet

[ecstatic] distraction **[redact]**
[glazed over] daze **[redact]**
[happy] ending **[redact]**

oh muddy the waters
oh vessel
oh chimera divine

all those roiling boys
pumping deep in the belly
one or two in particular
thrilling their pipes
at such cosmetic endeavour

psych out

[don't mention the]
[never mention the]

[women]

(if I move faster than you can see,
may I change my matter?)

Football boots

On the Mound, the three Graces simper.
Down Middle Meadow Walk,
a tilting clatter of pre-teen boys
football boots clicking like high heels
engrossed in gossip.
Full of self-conscious pride,
mirth, splendour.

Joy

Joy is not a cheerful brittle best girl voiced by America's
 sweetheart.
Joy is a fat toddler with a permanently dirty face.
Joy eats dirt.
Joy waddles about.
Joy cannot see what is on the kitchen table.
Joy crawls under gorse bushes. Joy draws blood.
Joy likes company but does not seek it out.
Joy likes to sit alone on park benches.
Once, Joy bit the head off a pigeon.
Joy often laughs and cries at the same time.
Joy does not know what love is.
Joy avoids deserts but likes to look at cloudless night skies, shoals of
 fish and the movement of beaded curtains.
Joy has seen a river but not the ocean.
Joy has eaten fish and chips from a bin.
Joy made best friends with a snail and then sat on it.
Each morning, Joy laughs as she brushes her teeth for the first time.
Joy does not ask to be picked up and held.
Joy never wears clothes.
Once a pelican tried to fit Joy in its beak and carry her back to the
 nest. Joy laughed at the adventure and then smacked the
 heads of the baby birds together.
People are frightened of Joy.
Joy sticks dice from the gambling table up her nose.
Joy hangs off the tail of an elephant.

An accident-prone psychic visits the shortlist for the 2015 Turner Prize, dressed in a fur coat

Cold white cold
tile tracks tile
fur fingers fawn
the expensive pales
taupe mauve caramel
cocktail party cool
worth unmmeasured
riches unquantified
possessions unprized
banana slip split
immersive absence
stifling lack of consensus
precognition failing to see
reality unreal wired up
to light and warmth
and folk and bin collections
and the little piecemeal messes
that are a way to dream
and live and live

and a tap that hurts to…
DO NOT TOUCH
(but I'm thirsty)

a tap that hurts to…
DO NOT TOUCH
(but it's cold in here)

a tap that hurts to…
DO NOT
(too late)

Pigs and wolves

'Sometimes the Wolf is quiet. But now the Wolf is loose and ranging
and we are afraid of him.' – Naomi Mitchison, *The Fourth Pig*

Here we are again, back to the pigs and the wolves.
The pigs have been spoilt
and the lean, low nosed wolves are sniffing around.

Blow blow blow my house down.
All that sweet, soft, buttery goodness
hamstrung-up, and starting to spoil.

That sea-salt cure-all
lard-rubbed goodness
is starting to spoil.

Those grain-fed trotters,
cheese-doused haunches,
on the turn, rancid and exposed.

Under starlight, Europe's layered saints
crumble to icing sugar. Unheave Tararre, Domery,
Erysichthon from their straining places at the table.

In the yellowing grass –
in the yellow-eyed lope –
cry wolf cry

★★★

Ceres screamed out to the wilderness
and Fames – who has been biding
her scaly scurfy lipped time – has come to dwell in bellies.

As the foul vapours clear, uncovered is
the midden of offal, tallow candles,
raw cow's udder, barrels of apples,

the dismembered chomped-on leg of a fellow crewman
and a spat-out tail-tip all that's left
from those one hundred and seventy four live cats.

As the quivering flesh stills
all damp crackling and weeping fat,
those small, nifty wolves rise up from the cracks in the oak table.

In the yellowing grass –
in the yellow-eyed lope –
cry wolf cry –

fear of hunger eats itself in the end.

Elpenor in the basement

In the basement of the art college
Elpenor hangs forgotten.

Perpetual birdman, hands flapping and fluttering,
he mutters, dreaming over and over

of a rooftop in Greece and white sails
that he did not see being raised.

On that morning, in another corridor, red tiled
and warm, his companions talk in loud voices.

They are waiting for an audience.
They are performing *Some Distillations of Survival.*

A backdrop of tincture of lemons and of dust
presented in old washed bottles.

Stories that they have researched and revised,
combed over like scavengers on a beach. But it's tricky.

They do not yet understand failure.
They have survived nothing, except this.

No one comes. Casually, they rip apart
the work of their peers

kick around obscene stuffed nylon stockings
laughing, release an inflatable dolphin from a coffee jar

which is, in truth, saying nothing about anything
but has inexplicably won the artist a residency in Ghent.

They speak of the open world
how they are standing on the doorstep to freedom.

No one comes. The birdman stirs
in his sleep, cries out once.

Impatient now, they cast their posturing aside,
pour the failed performance down a plughole,

toss the pool toy from a casement window.
They set sail to a world not waiting to welcome them.

Tomorrow, the timbers of the ship
will be torn apart. Dull ties will be loosened

from shirt collars in late night city bars
and it will be years before they remember him.

Still balanced on the guttering edge
the one that no one noticed hadn't made it.

The ship sailed without him and still
he balances smiling nervously, thick gloss

of pale and clammy sweat. The lightbulbs
burn out one by one and his fluttering hands never tire,

as he cries *Hey! Hey! Wait for me!*
Look, I'm flying!

The last rhino

The craggy sorrow of the last Northern White male
rhinoceros, Sudan. The bewilderment in the hang

of that bouldering head
would break your heart and mine.

Chin tucked meekly without the full weight of horn
hacked and stumped, for his own safety

on the cracked glaze earth
of the National Park.

So alone, apart
– from the three armed sentries, trained

automatic rifles and the burst of static
from the watchtower

from the horn-embedded transmitters
and the silent alert hounds

and the black blank pupil of the drone ranging overhead
– so very alone. This last male rhino.

Sudan, the last Northern White male rhinoceros
– whose skin, actually a heavy greyish colour

is virtually indistinguishable from that of his cousin,
the Southern Black rhinoceros – doesn't know any of this.

Animals lack communication for things apart
from them in time or space

Except we think, for the waggle dance of the honey bee
and who knows how long that will last.

Oak trees in Stellenbosch

The oak trees of Stellenbosch
are dying, of course.

More accurately,
of a virus
of an unknown disease
of over proliferation
of the wrong climate
of being out of fashion
of never-should-have-been-here anyway
of old age
of time's-up
of make-room
of heart rot.

The birdmen of Istanbul

Only a bird that is caught
from freedom sings the best.

The neat double-wrapped boxes are hooked
overhead on olive tree branches
or onto the metal twigs extended from a modest cafe wall

right angled like a tensed forearm,
the fist clenched, veins rising to a throb.
The birdmen must reach up to stroke the bars

to delicately twitch apart lipped fabric,
shirts riding up
to expose the merest hint of skin.

They wait, leaning forward slightly
in intimate silence.
Time distilled to tension and distance.

Desire stems
from the disappearing twin tails
of hope and denial.

Yellow liquid noise erupts,
the curtailed trill and chirrup,
dual notes voluble, a swelling

to concerto, a falling away.
Covetousness burns
like a thirst after salt.

La poupee

Mm
Ma
Mama
Mamamamamama
Maaaaaaaaaaaaaaaaaa
Maaaaaaaaaaaaaaaaaaaaaaaaaaan

The doll has hit a bum note.
Has missed her grace notes.

Maaaaaaaaaaaaaaaaaaaaaan
Maaaan

The doll
is puppet
is vessel
is scarecrow
is marble
is rubber
is plastic
is fibreglass
is faceless
is orifice
is object
is pixels
is cover
is projection
is virtual
is silent
is stiff
is passive
is provocation
is tease
is doll
is girl
is mannequin.

My underwear was made of iron

On a street with chewing gum
welded to paving slabs
and rubbish bins and dogs
and dust and wire fences
and raindrops and men
like any street

A skirt
or a pair of breasts
or, let's say,
a crate of oranges
was slowly making its way

wearing a scold's bridle made of iron
and a witch's collar made of iron
with the metal spikes
facing both out and in
and a chastity belt made of iron
and a steel-boned corset
reined in tight.

A suit of rigid homespun armour
that clanked and drew attention
and held protection and rebuke
in each hand like the
severed fibreglass breasts of
a shopwindow mannequin
or a sliced forehead
or a broken jawbone.

What can't get out also
won't let anything in.

This is how we break butterflies
they said.

The crate of oranges kept walking
in its steel hide, kept walking.

I am Gigi Hadid's left elbow

I am Kubra Khademi's breastplate.
I am Grace O'Malley's canvas sails.
I am Monica Bellucci's eye contact.
I am Gina Miller's balls.

I am Josephine Baker's kneecaps.
I am Dorothy Parker's lemon slice.
I am Louise Bourgeois' arachnid joy.
I am Marina's knife.

I am Lee Miller's retina.
I am Claude Cahun's strongman suit.
I am Georgia O'Keeffe's open flowers.
I am Baroness Elsa von Freytag-Lorginghoven's HU HU!

I am Black Agnes' handkerchief.
I am Nina's plain gold ring.
I am Medea's jealousy.
I am Leoti Blaker's hatpin.

I am Lauren's instructions on how to whistle.
I am Amelia's dazzling flight.
I am Frida's spread kneed challenge.
I am Sylvia Plath's bite.

I am Wislawa's chained apes.
I am Patti's April Fool.
I am Annette Kellerman's bathing robe.
I am Saint Joan's refusal.

I am Sarah Maple's slapped face.
I am Kiki's broken smile.
I am Jennifer Frey's locker room.
I am Emilia's shaming guile.

I am Hillary's hard-fought challenge.
I am Cordelia's punishment.
I am Tank Girl's cigarette butt.
I am Ellen Ripley's bitchtalk.

I am Susan Ballion's pseudonym.
I am Liza's upturned palms.
I am Adrienne's voice through concrete
and I am Polly's 50 ft Queen.

Take Me to Market, Mother Dear
(a strategy of dissonance)

Lettuce prey sisters

and ask this of ourselves
do I know these wimmen?

> *not much of a mama you see not much of a dada either*
> *boom tish boom*

send miss ives back
send help at once
we are going to a dance

it's Hallowe'en sisters
and I'm late to the party
masked up in a guerrilla suit
still wearing those painted masks
get gorilla-ed up for the moral guardians girls

it's our polemic poemic fight
boxed-in ring and crocheted left hook
let's pussy riot before
they beam us up

> *We used to talk about...*

so we reflect on this
we reflect this

(if I took tiny shards of mirror and –
but we don't use mirrors so much these days
> *don't look too closely or you'll go blind doing that)*

I have been a child but not a mother.

Marie Stopes International has provided safe contraception worldwide
for 40 years did you know that Marie Stopes wrote love letters to Hitler
she did did you know that Marie Stopes opposed abortion did you know
that Marie Stopes cut her own son out of her will because he married a

woman with an eye defect did you know that in 1921 Marie Stopes wrote
about her Society for Constructive Birth Control and Racial Progress
that it existed to 'counteract the steady evil which has been growing for
a good many years of the reduction of the birth rate just on the part of
the thrifty, wise and well contented, and the generally sound members
of our community, and the reckless breeding from the C.3 end, and the
semi-feebleminded, the careless, who are proportionately increasing in
our community because of the slowing down of the birth rate at the other
end of the social scale. Statistics show that every year the birth rate from
the worst end of our community is increasing in proportion to the birth
rate at the better end, and it was in order to try to right that grave social
danger that I embarked upon this work' did you know that but they do
good work now they do such important work in her name now its difficult
when the ends justify the means still such a horror story you know
anyway
it's done now
let's look now
at their quiet disparate cleaver urgency
stuttered through the letterbox slit
their UR-GENCY
the UR-GENCY
the UR of it all
the UR UR URRRRR of it all

Few physical resource…many of them use old packaging…we recycle
lots of things. Ecological bunch!…not all of us…nor I think…nearly
impossible for all but a few…a bit more lots of things…lots and lot of
things…

UR…UR…UR

When, opposite, is the
MAGMA STYLE women art's explosion ITALIAN STYLE
Glory Glory Glory BOOM to the DAWN
magma eroding undermining subterranean spread

I disavow all soundness of mindfulness.
I'm just not sure I know you sisters
but I think you met my mother though
★★★

Sorry about the stuttering.
I'm jealous of your merry elastic bands

(what happens if we don't agree?)
                     CO OPERATE YOU MUST CO OPERATE

of your flying ducks
of the ducks you do not give
away on that egg yellow cover

(I'll look when I'm a mother)

This just isn't me but just because this isn't me doesn't mean it isn't
you and
you and you and her and them and her over there and here her here
and you
and sorry I am sorry
never sure what I'm to bring to the table
always was the jealous sort of fish

that old envy fit to poison any sort of dish

all this kitchen talk is making me queasy
holding my breath in a clenched fist here

let's take it outside
anywhere anywhere i don't care i don't care
take me out tonight
and love me Linder
in your pornographic meat suit
in the public thumping realm
and slap that sausage and cook that goose
shit cook that goose
shit we're back in the kitchen

goose in the kitchen oven
oh my Plath

★★★

Look, this, I promise.
I will spread my knees on subway trains.
Show 'em how wide and dark the tunnel is.

★★★

And I asked him
how was it to become a dadadadada so young?
He told me the first time he felt his father
look on him as a man was when their eyes met
over his son's head crooked in his 18 year old elbow

And he was worked and pried screaming fingers
from nursery fences to be a good dadadadada
and god I love the way he folds clothes

I've lived on my own air since I was 18 years old
two cuts to the bellysac my choice post-everything
and I'm not sure that I know you sisters
I think you met my mother though
but let's meet outside the malebox sisters
whisper stutter scream it from our outboxes sisters
make our own Hallowe'en masks from serial boxes and head out for
    the dance
I'll see you at the dance sisters
let's get through the letterbox
let's get postal my sisters
let's get post-al this shit.

The First Blast to Awaken Women Degenerate

'And therefore, I say, that of necessity it is that this monstiferous empire of women (which amongst all enormities that this day do abound upon the face of the whole earth, is most detestable and damnable) be openly revealed and plainly declared to the world, to the end that some may repent and be saved.'

(The First Blast of the Trumpet Against the Monstruous Regiment of Women – John Knox, 1558)

The trumpet sounds.

All the monkeys are grooming
themselves bald in the zoos

Women slither out from gutters
and under streetlamps

down from bedsits
and from behind garden fences

Foil sail unfolding irresistible as empty crisp packets
on pub table women

Women who sink a bottle of red
and rage with wine lips women

Fury unleashed women
in stamping, stomping

sweating hordes of women
ranks amassing women

Give me gorilla women and bear women
penguin women and wolf hound women

blue whale women and badger women
yeti, yak and bison women

Give me caribou women and bone women
bite back beefy women

not your bird women
least of all your sparrow, crow or wren women

but flamingo women and peacock women

eagle women and pelican women

Give me unnatural women
deranged women

moving, drumming
howling women

Give me mobs of women
chow down on misery women

seismic cunt women
bloody pushy women

like a 2 a.m. army's march
through the veins women

Give me ruling women
and yelling women

Give me unsilent
unwatchful women

Give me monstrous women
on the pavements of

Cologne women
London women
Tahrir Square women
Belfast women
Stockholm women
Cape Town women
Bangalore women
Glasgow women

before the second trumpet sounds

before the monkeys can groom themselves bare and repent

before the streets can fall dark and silent and damned

please

give me
my monstrous regiment
of women

Oh my fathers

Where did you leave your women, Ulster?
In the kitchens, at the sinks,
paring down, paring down
to the red sore quick of their nails.

By the time it got bad, the mills
had already been shut.
The women to lose
their duchess flax complexions

their hard-earned holler.
To keep indoors, bake wee buns
millionaire's shortbread, scones
for the trestle tables down at the Field.

*

Behind a nervous blackbird trilling,
brushed bowlers and white gloves step out.
Fingers splayed stiff on wooden poles,
orange and purple rigid with the oul brocade.

But oh my fathers, you have told our story badly.
And I will heave my heart into my mouth
and berate you for that stubborn, stupid pride
with which you have cuckolded yourselves.

I love you as salt,
bitter and vital,
left in tattered glittering ribbons
looping on a shore that the tide left long ago.

But the last time I stepped down onto the docks
I saw ghosts of myself on every street corner.
One, older, stopped and turned towards me,
her mouth opened in an unbirthed howl.

(Untitled) with MGD

Write on yourself tonight
and you may find something on your hands.
All the tiny barbs and tripwires
that only the twist of a lemon could give away.

I fell asleep.
Neither of us being the women we once were
calling me young lady
hooking your gaze in the 3 a.m. chippie
like you're a prime cod fillet.

Bare your ankles and your teeth
on the same day.
At last, grasping the rope of your bony knuckles
we will sink or swim.
The latitude you choose to live in,
it tells me what you are.

Like all the ripe shadows that scared me
on the way home
a fat tabby, a glass bottle
the last cab before dawn.

Those damned gazelles and thoroughbreds
high on the thrill of the chase.
Stop excusing yourself and bite it
hook line and sinker will pull you up.

Sweat till the devil loses your scent.
Chew on the bitter leaves of my silence
the full name of your nemesis.
Hold your nerves like steel.

I've got the medicine
the healing spell
Madonna, we love you! Get up!
I, too, have made it through the wilderness.

When the pebbles in your shoes
become seven league springs,
the bruises will be gold in your stride.

Bury me at sea

She said

I left civil twilight a while ago
to hunt for the North
and isn't that the cosmic kicker,
that it's never a fixed point,
the one you're looking for?

Tried kelp farming once.
No go.
When I reached the shale,
I kept going,
struck out to swallow the world.
My eyes were always bigger
than my stomach.

Couldn't be shot
of the clan quick enough.
In my haste, gob agape,
I let the sea pour in.
My tongue dried out.

I'd heard that sucking pebbles
quenches a thirst
but failed to see they'd tumble
from maw to gut,

the rattle of them capsized me,
turned me turtle.

Then my country,
still shackled to my ankle,
my cannonball and my ship's wheel,
my ammunition and my steerage,
did the rest.

Never even made it
past the harbour mouth.

Remain mistress of your craft.
The vessel yours and yours alone.
This belly's only good for stones.

Luss

We don't mind where we go
as long
as it is away.

The name hooked us,
so irresistibly strung between lust
and loss. Kiss, too, if we wanted.

One of those hung grey days,
heavy, the hills burnt orange
and not yet the full chilly barren

strangeness of the Highlands.
It should be picturesque
but the trees are dying.

Our planned lochside wander thwarted
by padlocked fences on both sides.
Curtailed, bone weary, meaning slips.

One inscription claims the name
from the French *lys;* another,
twenty yards down the road, from the Gaelic *luss.*

Before the herbs and the saints
Clachan Dubh:
the dark village brought to light.

We idly stalk the old couple
round the hogback stones, him proud
in expensive tartan and frailer than he hopes he looks.

Outwith the sanctified plots,
sagging yellow polka dot cellophane
holds brownish water, dead stalks

ribboned to trees like hostages of memory.
We trespass on grief – as I do here –
amongst wrenched charred wood,

black-forked, cracked and tiny fires.

Further onto the Glebe, we trample
past BBQ-scorched tables,
tip-tilted in the flooded turf.

Yellow and red pops of colour, blemished
sickly rotten black up close.
Rowan trees decked with cards like Christmas trees.

It's a pilgrimage site.
Exhortations to walk gently
upon any gods earth, upon ourselves.

Armenia, Assisi,
St Albans, Amritsar
and Luss.

Nothing really helps.
The birds leave those berries alone.

That night, I'm sticky with blood, of course,
and our neat room is comfortable and airless.
Your casual heavy arm slung over my chest

customary as a lifebelt. The usual intimate dialogue
between our knees silenced by the too-hot bloody throb.
I crack the door, suck in cold.

What use is away?
To walk and walk the earth
and still those worn cellophane strings

and re-written labels,
blind faith to shift
from darkness to light

and we return
to those lumpen shingled stones
compressing the dirt, holding down the dead.

I did not see the heron leave

The sand was breathing. Dirty hoppers
flicking frantic on bare ankles
the lugworms starspread at dusk
excreting perfect twisting grains.

I stepped on their leavings
as cheerfully as children
calling out how many they crush
one, five, twenty, eighty nine.

Sand at the shore like you wouldn't believe.
Heaps and heaps that we shifted
from spot to spot every summer
with plastic buckets and wooden handled spades.

Earlier at the cemetery
facing a hard bright sea
we stacked your coffin
in your husband's grave.

Sand at the shore like you wouldn't believe.
Bright emerald seaweed plastered over rocks
and the burnt neon pink of the sky orange
empty like you wouldn't believe.

The sand breathed. My foot brushed
a sodden buried sweater, jumped
at the thought of conger eel
or dogfish.

You would have laughed at the fancy

with your lipstick
and your faith
and your sense.

The sand was breathing like you wouldn't believe.
Dirty hoppers flicking frantic on bare skin,
The heron had left unseen. Just the old
familiar empty mackerel sky.

We brought it to the sea to air

We brought it to the sea to air,
to take the salt cure.

We propped it up to peer
through the smeared crust
of the perspex ferry windows.

We laid it out on harbour walls
and in thin-mattressed
guesthouse bedrooms.

We sauntered along promenades
held it up to watch the birds shoal
above the drag of waves.
We wound it up Grieveship Brae
and looked down upon the island.

We tried to stroke it smooth
unrise prickled hackles
unruffle worried feathers
pat down raised scales
till all was silver and rainbows

and still it lay there
gasping.

On the beach, we performed mouth to mouth
until we could no longer tell
if those were salt crystals or sand grains
crunching at the corners of our lips.

We fed it ham sandwiches and chips.
Though we couldn't say it
we'd taken it on a guilt trip.

Better slipped into the water
between the pier and the fishing boat.
Better pecked out by gulls,
gutted with the mackerel catch.
Better hosed into a tank of crabs,
smothered by kelp,
lacerated by barnacles,
Better sucked under quicksand.
Better smashed by a standing stone.

Better the roof finally falls to crush its skull.
the ribs picked clean by bone beetles

than to lie there gasping.

Finally, we let it go out to sea.
Watched it nudge aside a crisp packet
beneath the sign
for the Eventide Club.

The rule of twelths

this cannot be measured, this must be loved
(Van Gogh on Hans Christian Andersen)

I misremember knots
seabirds
the parts of yachts

confuse the order of the shipping forecast
the symptoms of the Beaufort scale
the classes of lifeboats

and I have misinformed you
about all these things
with confidence and clear eyes

– holding back the lie from my gaze
needing to give you some empirical account
of myself, some worth –

but I taught you the rule of twelths right.
A rule of thumb, no more or less,
but marvellous to us all the same

that we call on when we need to
rest our heads against the ebb and flow

the same soaring sine
curve of surging water
over which all tides bend their backs.

Lux

Some days are light days
and some days are heavy days
some days fast
days
and some
days
slow days

there is no old light
no new light
no curious light
nor hopeful light
no fearful light
nor careful light
no light
more loving or indifferent
than any other light

★★★

Just after sunrise
the old woman nurses porridge,
waiting for the world
to catch up.

Sees the street clean and bright
as in a sea light
light set at odd angles
a broken birdwing light.

Not yet dust-kicked-up-by-day light.
She remembers coffee and mangoes,
other breakfasts in hotter lights.
Everything happens for a season.

She watches a young couple creep home
skulk through shadows
like airplanes caught behind the dateline
forever chasing dawn.

Down on the pavement
the girl mouths *blinker me*
and he cups her temples
palms warm against her hair.

They'll be Jack-Go-To-Bed-At-Noons
the world circled
in their eyes –
hers blue, his green.

Eyelashes like blinds
drawing down
cosy as darkness dancing.
Everything happens for a season.

Across town the ancient dancer

Across town, she wraps
the past around her like a blanket
and rocks spidery feathery
in and out of light

Beneath the lovers on the bridge
salmon swim in silent flashing fury.
Look she says *there is a view.*
He raises his head obediently
from the nuzzle of her neck.
They have not yet started to lie
to one another in language,
are playing dress-up from another time.
Red lipstick, a man's woollen overcoat,
and cracked leather shoes.

Across town, she feels
the barbs of a million lilliputian connections.
She was born in thunder and silence.
Inside her there are mountains
and still she rocks
in and out of light.

The teacher is home, footsore and cramped,
and tired of sink mould. With rictus razorclam claws,
she rakes through soil, bares her teeth to the world.
Wildeyed and wired, she remembers the warmth
of the hardknuckled whisper of a man
who told her jokes to feel the laugh quake between her legs.
With the last of her salary, she has bought seeds,
potting compost, the hope of green things.

Across town, she flinches,
rearranges her visage serene
and smooth as a death mask
and continues to rock
in and out of light.

The engine rattles dark windows,
skirts the edges of the town.
Cheerful on carriage seats, the undertaker
and his wife pass a flask of tea between them.
This trip's paid for because I've had three funerals
this week. The dead are keeping us alive!
She sniffs happily. Not bad people.
They are merely content.

> *Across town, she remembers*
> *traintracks and snowfall, juddering eyes*
> *ticking off fenceposts, the deep slots*
> *of the cattle boxes racketing on.*
> *Her blue eyes flick open, filmy, close.*
> *The movement slows but never ceases*
> *in and out of light.*

In a basement, the hungry man with shattered teeth
squats frightened, gradually becomes hurricane.
He dreams of sacrificial legs of lamb,
splendid glistening fat, sodden and roasted.
Scrambling out to the night, he gobs
in the street, rips off his fingernails on bin lids,
scrabbles for something to bloat with.
Culverts lie across his path like dinosaur spines,
the lines of the place cracked and broken
the crevasses of his poor and raging hands.

> *Across town, she straightens*
> *in her chair, puts her spine to the mountains,*
> *drapes over the forests, the valley.*
> *Over the snowfall and the traintracks.*
> *She rocks faster, the shadow of the chair swings*
> *across the attic wall,*
> *in and out of light.*

The politician pulls up the collar of his overcoat, turns his head.
The young lovers leave the lamplit bridge, and climb the cobbles.
The teacher massages her feet, slips into snowboots, breathes deep.
The hungry man makes his pilgrimage and dares – just once – to
     raise his eyes.
The undertaker and his wife offer around their flask of tea.
Together, they stand beneath the attic window

in the snow and lamplight,
paying homage to resilience.
Nothing is fixed,
nor should it be.
The shadow moves
across the attic wall,
in and out of light.

The village blood bank

I go looking for blood banks
not in the large cities
but in small villages
and I wonder how every village
knows how to give
just enough blood

the way they know
that there is one person
in the village
who is the strongest
who would pull the truck from the river
and another who always has a pot on the stove
and another who is the kindest
and yet another who will unexpectedly
rally the crowd
when the hour comes.

Girvan

Whit's yer hurry?

That dirty great sea beastie Ailsa Craig
waiting to finally lumber up evilly
scattering barnacles and dripping bladderwrack.

Birds with deadly little beaks
and old bulls in a field
wrinkled like a giant's knuckles.

The sand dunes push back to the mountains.
Chins dug in, eyes down.
The rocks in those hurried cramped layers
as the sea repeatedly slaps them back.

And for all that, still rip-roaring against the wind,
Frankie the Slug,
Jodie Pie + Kimbo Smee
whitewash the rocks.

Haste ye back.

Time difference

We discuss things
that might fund a move –
the sale of a kidney
a lung
a cornea
a lip.

**

I've half the day gone by the time you're up
or am bleary and oxter-deep in a bottle
waiting for you to finish homework, bathtime.
No wonder we feel insubstantial.

**

The first time I flew to you,
the plane passed over a graveyard
before hitting the runway.
I flew towards that dawn in a tin tube
full of strangers and thin air.

**

In Dunbar, we saw birds using lobster pots
as voluntary bird cages.
Ramshackle stacked towerblocks,
all sun and air and chirruped song.

**

Out on Belhaven, the sand squidged out dryness
underfoot. I watched like it was someone else's foot
squeezing out the water, then paused,
really dug in to see how far it might shift.

★★

Driving out from Halifax,
leaving thunderclouds, pressure, horizon.
19 years of listening to Van's Astral Weeks,
dreaming of the way that we were –
that we wanted to be.

★★

In the dark, watching the old poet
with the lion hair
You'll look like her.
You recognise more of me
than I do.

★★

An ear or an eye.
Just leave us one each
and we'll make it whole again.
Pound by pound by pound of flesh,
down to the bone, start with the bone,
the marrow.

★★

I still sometimes dry my horses
instead of my hair,
request donkeys instead of mussels,
hunt shoes in the forest
and feel my tongue retreat
in reddening cheeks
but we manage –
	Je te manque –
and I no longer miss myself.

Notes

The following poems have been published elsewhere:
'Who wants a home?' (originally *In Residence*), 'Radio Orkney', 'The five o'clock poem', 'An accident-prone psychic...' and 'Lux' (originally 'Light') were all originally written as Poet In Residence for BBC Scotland, 2015. 'Ling Chi' was written for *Neu Boots & Pantisocracies* anthology, curated by Bill Herbert and Andy Jackson, 2014. 'The Official Line' was commissioned by Edinburgh Art Festival in August 2016, as part of the Dazzle Ship project and 'Signal' pamphlet. 'Take Me to Market, Mother Dear' (a strategy of dissonance) was part of the contentworkproduceform project in autumn 2016: a collective of Scottish poets co ordinated by JL Williams to write and respond to the 1970s feminist postal art project, and commissioned by Sophia Hao at Cooper Gallery Dundee. 'Bury me at sea' was written for the 2015 'Territories' project co ordinated by the Edinburgh International Book Festival and Maison de la Poesie (Montreal), in which female Innu and Scotland based writers collaborated and responded to one another's work.

Acknowledgements

'Problems to Sharpen The Young' (I, II and III) owe their initial premise to Alcuin's 9th century text.

'Runaways' owes thanks to Matthew McCrum, for explaining the difference between celestial orphans and celestial runaways to me. You're right, brother mine. It does flow better. Love you always. 'Tomato Sonata' is inspired by the art project of the same name by John Gilbert, Marcus Patton in Belfast in the 1970s (with thanks to Marilynn Richtarik's biography of Stewart Parker for enlightening me, and Peggy Hughes for tracking down the only photographic record we could find of it.) 'For the want of a nail' is owed to the man who releases a nail to a helium-filled balloon each day of the siege in Aleppo. 'Joy' and 'The village blood bank' owe a debt to the marvellous Caroline Bird. 'Elpenor in the basement' owes a debt to the painting by Christos Borokos in the National Gallery in Nafplion, Greece, and to Matina Goga for showing it to me. More about 'The birdmen of Istanbul' in the documentary by Ali Naki Tez, and the article in Colours Magazine by Maria Sturm and Cemre Yesil. 'My underwear was made of iron' is dedicated to Kubra Khademi's armour performance in Kabul (available on YouTube, 8 minutes). '(Untitled) with MGD' was a collaborative online photographic project with Margarida Jorge in February 2015. 'I did not see the heron leave' is for Sadie McCrum. 'Across town the ancient dancer' owes a debt to the film piece in the Imperial War Museum North in Manchester, 'Will you dance for me?' by Ori Gersht, featuring the dancer Yehudit Arnon (85 years old).

Thanks

My thanks to all at Freight Books for publishing this collection, and to Robyn Marsack for patient, meticulous and insightful editing. It was a pleasure and an honour to work with you on this. My thanks also to Ryan Van Winkle for a challenging, needed last-minute close read, to Dave Coates and Harry Giles for help with specific poems, and to Hannah McGill, Francesca Beard, Ross Sutherland and Liz Lochhead for taking the time to read and offer words of encouragement. I am indebted to various residencies, voyages, and opportunities that have been provided over the past few years by Creative Scotland, the Scottish Poetry Library, the Edinburgh International Book Festival, the British Council, the Callum MacDonald Award and the Michael Marks Foundation, BBC Scotland, Coastword, the Scottish Book Trust and the Robert Louis Stevenson Foundation, and the marvellous, vibrant spoken word community in Scotland. Finally, in addition to those already mentioned, thank you, from the bottom of my messy heart, to all who have been friends over the past few years, with your patience, your sharing of tea and wine, your generosity. Neither this nor I would be here without yous. To: the Authentic Artist community, Abby Boultbee, Kath Burlinson, Chris & Mary Cunningham-Siggs, Caroline Evens, the Forest Cafe, Miriam Gamble & Peter Mackay, James Harding, Cataline Iordache, Margarida Jorge, Billy Liar, Jenny Lindsay, Paul Oertel and Nancy Spanier, Chris Scott, Biff Smith, Chris Thorpe, Sophia Walker, Johnny Wells, and Anna Porubcansky and Ewan Downie at Company of Wolves. To Mum and Dad, always, for your big dreams and your stubborn selves. To Jonathan Lamy, for the joy and for the calm, with love from the core of me.